Mountains
INSIDE OUT

James Bow

CRABTREE
Publishing Company
www.crabtreebooks.com

Author: James Bow
Publishing plan research
 and series development: Reagan Miller
Editors: Sarah Eason, Jennifer Sanderson
 and Shirley Duke
Proofreaders: Katie Dicker, Wendy Scavuzzo
Editorial director: Kathy Middleton
Design: Paul Myerscough
Cover design: Paul Myerscough
Photo research: Jennifer Sanderson
Production coordinator and
 Prepress technician: Tammy McGarr
Print coordinator: Katherine Berti

Written and designed for Crabtree Publishing
 by Calcium Creative

Photo Credits:

t=Top, bl=Bottom Left, br=Bottom Right

Dreamstime: Estavanik: p 1, p. 18–19; Getty Images: p. 27t; Nature PL: Gavin Maxwell: p. 21b; Visuals Unlimited: p. 11b; Shutterstock: A Lein: p. 25b; Elliotte Rusty Harold: p. 12–13; Fedor Korolevskiy: p. 4–5; Fedor Selivanov: p. 26–27; Filip Fuxa: p. 1b, p. 19b; Galyna Andrushko: p. 6–7; Marekuliasz: 8–9; Pecold: p. 24–25; Pierre Leclerc: p. 28; Protasov AN: p. 10–11; Robert Cicchetti: p. 14–15, p. 16–17; Rweisswald: p. 20–21; S.R. Maglione: p. 3; Tom Grundy: p. 17b; Tom Reichner: p. 9b; Volodymyr Burdiak: p. 28–29; Worldswildlifewonders: p. 13t; Wikimedia Commons: Donald Hobern: p. 15t; Penjgo: p.23b; Yun Stock Photos: Tomo: p. 22–23.

Cover: Shutterstock: Daniel Prudek; MicheleBoiero (br).

Library and Archives Canada Cataloguing in Publication

Bow, James, 1972-, author
    Mountains inside out / James Bow.

(Ecosystems inside out)
Includes index.
Issued in print and electronic formats.
ISBN 978-0-7787-1498-9 (bound).--
ISBN 978-0-7787-1502-3 (pbk.).--
ISBN 978-1-4271-7654-7 (html).--
ISBN 978-1-4271-7658-5 (pdf)

    1. Mountain ecology--Juvenile literature. 2. Mountain
animals--Juvenile literature. I. Title.

QH541.5.M65B68 2015   j577.5'3   C2014-907851-X
                                               C2014-907852-8

Library of Congress Cataloging-in-Publication Data

CIP available at the Library of Congress

Crabtree Publishing Company
www.crabtreebooks.com   1-800-387-7650

Printed in Canada/022015/IH20141209

Published in Canada
Crabtree Publishing
616 Welland Ave.
St. Catharines, Ontario
L2M 5V6

Published in the United States
Crabtree Publishing
PMB 59051
350 Fifth Avenue, 59th Floor
New York, New York 10118

Published in the United Kingdom
Crabtree Publishing
Maritime House
Basin Road North, Hove
BN41 1WR

Published in Australia
Crabtree Publishing
3 Charles Street
Coburg North
VIC, 3058

Contents

What Is an Ecosystem?

Plants and animals need many things to survive. They need sunshine, clean air, soil, and water, as well as temperatures that are neither too hot, nor too cold. These nonliving things are called **abiotic factors**. Plants and animals also depend on each other for food. They are each other's **biotic factors**. An **ecosystem** is made up of **organisms**, the environment in which they live, and their **interrelationships**.

How Big Are Ecosystems?

An ecosystem can be as small as a rock, or it can stretch for thousands of miles. A **biome** is a large geographical area that contains similar plants, animals, and environments. Tundras, rain forests, grasslands, oceans, and deserts are biomes.

What Is a Mountain Ecosystem?

Mountains are places where Earth's surface rises above the area around it. They can form when the actions of a volcano build up a cone of rock. Mountains are also created when the movement of Earth's **plates** crumple its surface, and push it upward. The higher up a mountain you are, the colder the air becomes. This affects the amount of moisture that can fall on the mountain. The temperatures on a mountain and the amount of rainfall it receives determine what can live and grow there. The height of a mountain also affects its ecosystem.

Let's explore the mountain ecosystems of the world. We will look at each ecosystem as a whole, then explore one part of it further.

What Is a System?

A system is a group of separate parts that work together for a purpose. Living things exist in an ecosystem to help them survive. A healthy ecosystem has many different types of animals and plants living together, all having their needs met. These organisms depend on each other. If one part of the ecosystem changes or fails, others can be affected.

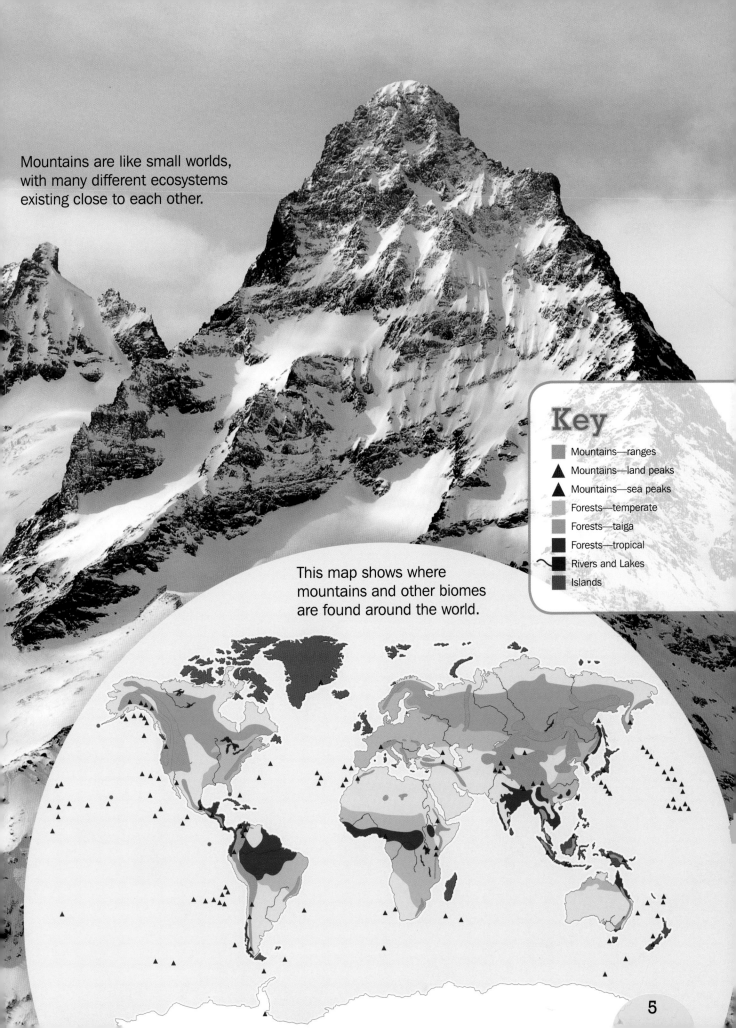

Mountains are like small worlds, with many different ecosystems existing close to each other.

This map shows where mountains and other biomes are found around the world.

Key

- Mountains—ranges
- ▲ Mountains—land peaks
- ▲ Mountains—sea peaks
- Forests—temperate
- Forests—taiga
- Forests—tropical
- Rivers and Lakes
- Islands

Energy in Ecosystems

Organisms need energy. This energy comes from the sun, and is spread through the ecosystem as food. This is known as a **food chain** or a **food web**. Within it, organisms play one of three roles: producer, consumer, or decomposer.

Moving Food Energy

Producers are organisms that make their own food from sunlight. Through a process called photosynthesis, plants, **algae**, and **bacteria** use **chlorophyll** to turn the sun's energy and **carbon dioxide** into sugar. The process releases oxygen, a gas that most animals need to take in to release energy from their food. The plants also get **nutrients** from the soil so that they can grow.

Some organisms cannot produce food from sunlight. They get their food by eating plants, algae, or other organisms that eat plants or algae. These organisms are called consumers. Herbivores are animals that eat only plants, carnivores eat herbivores or other carnivores, and omnivores eat both plants and animals.

Decomposers, such as bacteria and **fungi**, eat dead plants and animals. They break them down and return the nutrients to the soil. Producers grow by using nutrients from the soil or water around them, and food made by photosynthesis, allowing the food chain to begin again. Decomposition slows down when temperatures get cold. In the colder parts of a mountain, fewer dead organisms are broken down, which limits the nutrients in the food chain.

Keeping Healthy

Healthy food chains include different organisms. The variety of plant and animal life in an ecosystem is called **biodiversity**. If one part of the food chain is weakened, the ecosystem can fail.

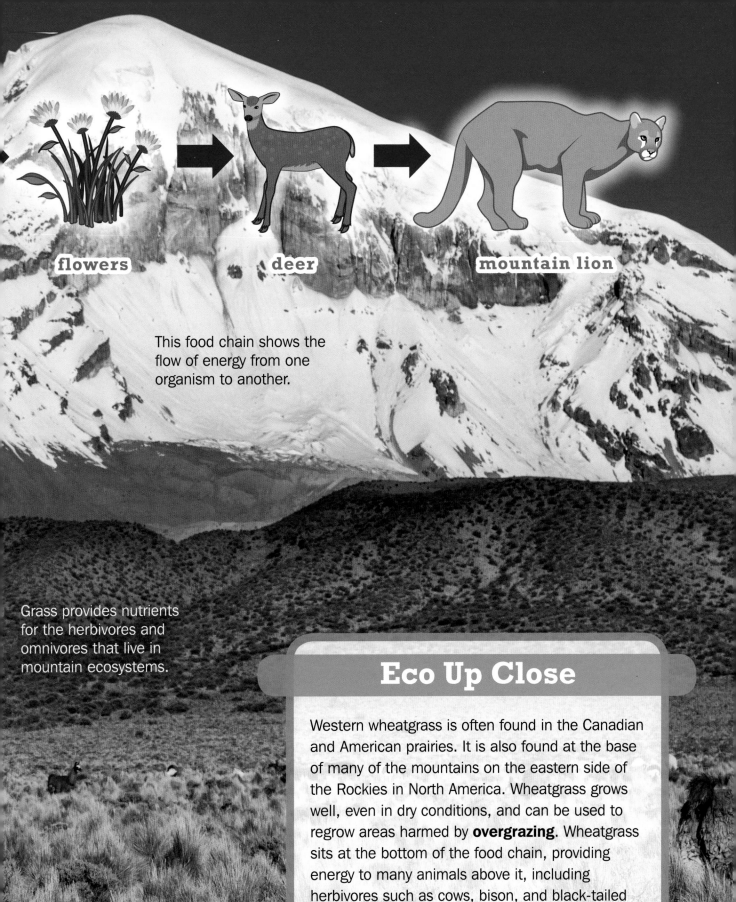

flowers

deer

mountain lion

This food chain shows the flow of energy from one organism to another.

Grass provides nutrients for the herbivores and omnivores that live in mountain ecosystems.

Eco Up Close

Western wheatgrass is often found in the Canadian and American prairies. It is also found at the base of many of the mountains on the eastern side of the Rockies in North America. Wheatgrass grows well, even in dry conditions, and can be used to regrow areas harmed by **overgrazing**. Wheatgrass sits at the bottom of the food chain, providing energy to many animals above it, including herbivores such as cows, bison, and black-tailed prairie dogs.

The Foothills

The lowest part of a mountain or a mountain range is sometimes known as the foothills. Examples include the foothills of the Rocky Mountains in North America, the Margalla near the Himalayas in Pakistan, and the Italian Piedmont region near the European Alps. These hills rise up from the area of land known as the plane, which surrounds the mountain. Parts of a mountain lower than 2,953 feet (900 m) above sea level are called **transition zones**. These share some of the features of the ecosystem that borders the mountain, as well as the mountain itself.

Over the Mountain

As a mountain grows, air and water work to wear down the mountain through a process called **weathering**. In this process, air and water blow or flow across rock, knocking off small pieces. When these weathered particles are moved by wind and water, this is called **erosion**. Water that gets into the cracks of rock can freeze in winter, and as the ice grows bigger, it can break rocks apart. Gradually, these smaller pieces of rock turn to sand and **silt**, which are carried down the mountain in streams and fast-moving rivers.

A lot of the sand and silt carried by mountain streams and rivers is dumped, or deposited, around the base of the mountain. There, it forms low, rolling hills.

The silt or sand-rich soil offers a **fertile** place for plants to grow. Mountain streams in the low hills also provide water, which may be harder to find farther from the mountain. This feeds the food chain and attracts animals from farther downstream. For example, the Rocky Mountain foothills in Colorado provide a **habitat** for Monarch butterflies, bald eagles, and mule deer.

People live at the foothills of many mountains. The land is flat and the soil is fertile, which is good for farming.

Eco Up Close

The Shiras moose is a **subspecies** of the moose. It is found in Washington, Oregon, Idaho, Montana, Utah, Colorado, and British Columbia. It has the smallest body and antlers of all the North American moose. Like other moose, the Shiras is a herbivore. It eats leaves, shoots, and fruits. Although the moose is prey for wolves and brown bears, its long legs help it escape. It can easily walk across rivers and push through snow. It can run at speeds of up to 34 miles per hour (55 kph). This moose climbs mountains in summer to avoid insects that bite, and returns to lower and warmer parts of the mountains in the fall.

Shiras moose

Montane Forests

Higher than 2,953 feet (900 m) above sea level, temperatures drop. This forces water vapor in the air to **condense** and drop its moisture as rain. In **temperate** climates, the summers are warm and the winters are cold. Examples of mountains with temperate climates include the Alps in Europe, the Appalachians in eastern North America, and the Rocky and Cascade Mountains in northwestern North America.

Temperate Trees

In temperate climates, the rain feeds mountain streams and allows forests to grow. The trees of these forests are usually **coniferous** and include pine, fir, cedar, and cypress trees. Coniferous trees have waxy, needle-like leaves that have adapted to the colder temperatures by providing a smaller area for the tree to lose heat and water. The pointy shape of coniferous trees lets snow slide off them. This ensures their branches do not break.

Tough Trees

The aspen is a mountain tree that is not coniferous, but **deciduous**. It grows well in cool summers and drops its leaves to reduce energy loss in winter. It is found in the northern part of the northern hemisphere at elevations of 5,000 to 12,000 feet (1,524 to 3,658 m). This tree does not grow well in shade. Forest fires can help young aspens grow, as they are able to survive the flames better than other plants due to their ability to grow from shoots rising from their roots. The fires clear weaker plants and trees from the mountain forest, which allows more sunshine to reach the young aspen trees.

Eco Focus

We get a lot of our electricity by building **dams** over fast-moving mountain streams to generate hydroelectricity. Generating power this way does not burn fossil fuels. When fossil fuels are burned, they release **greenhouse gases** that cause **climate change**. However, dams can get in the way of salmon migration. How could this affect the local ecosystem? How could this affect ecosystems downstream, too?

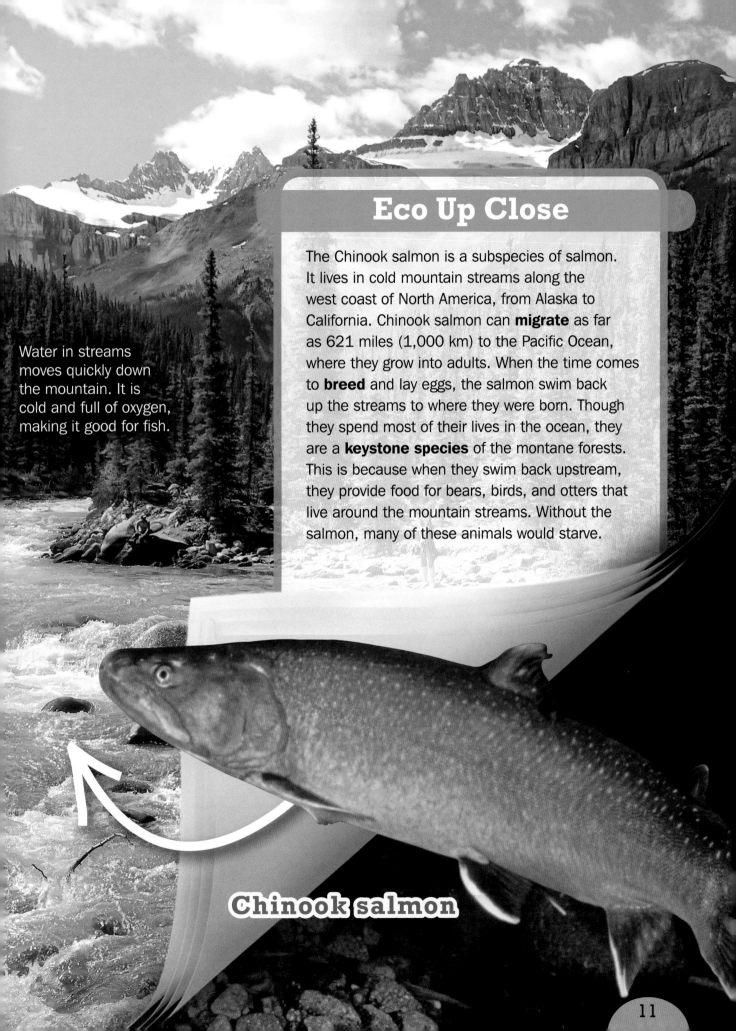

Eco Up Close

The Chinook salmon is a subspecies of salmon. It lives in cold mountain streams along the west coast of North America, from Alaska to California. Chinook salmon can **migrate** as far as 621 miles (1,000 km) to the Pacific Ocean, where they grow into adults. When the time comes to **breed** and lay eggs, the salmon swim back up the streams to where they were born. Though they spend most of their lives in the ocean, they are a **keystone species** of the montane forests. This is because when they swim back upstream, they provide food for bears, birds, and otters that live around the mountain streams. Without the salmon, many of these animals would starve.

Water in streams moves quickly down the mountain. It is cold and full of oxygen, making it good for fish.

Chinook salmon

Cloud Forests

The height, or elevation, of a mountain is more important to its climate than its **latitude**. Latitude is where something is on the planet in relation to the equator or the poles. Mountains that are closer to the equator are warmer than mountains that are closer to the poles. The tropical rain forests found on these mountains are often called cloud forests.

As different as the ecosystems are on a mountain, they are all connected. The water caught by the cloud forests flows downhill, bringing water to the lower elevations.

A Foggy Forest

Cloud forests are found higher up the mountain than temperate montane forests. They exist between about 4,921 and 11,483 feet (1,500 and 3,500 m) above sea level. These forests are often covered by clouds or fog. Examples of cloud forests include the Santa Elena Cloud Forest in Costa Rica and Mount Cargill in New Zealand. Some of the forests on the mountains near the coast of British Columbia have also been called cloud forests.

Rare Air

The wet conditions of cloud forests are good for **mosses** and ferns. The forest's high elevation means it has low oxygen levels. The lack of oxygen slows decomposers as they break down dead plants and animals. As a result, the soil of cloud forests has a lot of peat, which is made up of dead plant material. Peat holds moisture well, but does not have many nutrients. This means that the trees in a cloud forest are often smaller than those of other forests.

Cloud forests make up just one percent of the forests of the world, but they have a big effect on the ecosystems around them. The leaves of the trees catch moisture, allowing more of it to condense from the foggy air than would otherwise fall as rain. As a result, this extra water makes its way into lakes and rivers farther down the mountain.

Eco Up Close

The quetzal lives in the mountains of Central America, from southern Mexico to northern Panama. It migrates from the lower parts of mountains to cloud forests where it nests and breeds. The quetzal eats insects, small frogs, and lizards. Quetzals have a **mutualistic relationship** with the laurel tree. Quetzals eat the tree's fruits whole, and the seeds are scattered through their droppings. Trees grow from the seeds, spreading through the ecosystem.

quetzal

Alpine Grasslands

At around 9,843 feet (3,000 m) above sea level, air temperatures cool to a point where trees cannot grow. Above this treeline, grasses and **shrubs** are more common. This environment is known as an Alpine grassland. It is found in mountain ranges around the world, from the Highveld grasslands of South Africa and the Australian Alps to the Central Andean Puna in South America.

Unlike regular grasslands, most alpine grasslands are not flat. Plants and animals have to adapt to the rugged terrain.

Nowhere to Hide

The animals that live in Alpine grasslands have to change, or **adapt**, to a number of challenges. Compared with other grasslands, Alpine grasslands are smaller. There is not as much food to eat, and there are fewer places to hide. It is colder and the air is thinner. Although some Alpine grassland animals are similar to animals found on the larger grasslands below the mountains, they tend to be smaller. For example, the mountain zebra of the South African Highveld is shorter than the common grassland zebra of Africa. The **predators** found there, such as the Ethiopian wolf of the Ethiopian Highlands, can also be smaller.

Eco Focus

Mountain ecosystems can be very small compared with other ecosystems. Plants and animals that have adapted to a particular mountain ecosystem might not be able to survive if conditions change. What other ecosystems can you think of that might also be vulnerable to sudden change? How would these other ecosystems compare with mountain ecosystems?

bogong moth

Eco Up Close

The bogong moth is a night-flying moth that lives in southeastern Australia. It has a wingspan of 2 inches (5 cm). The caterpillars hatch out of eggs during the winter and eat a variety of plants before going into a cocoon and coming out as moths. As spring turns to summer, thousands of moths make a 1,864 mile (3,000 km) migration south to caves in the grasslands of the Australian Alps, to avoid the extreme heat. Farmers hate the caterpillars because they eat their crops. City dwellers dislike the swarms of moths that pass through, get distracted by lights, and become stuck in homes. However, the moths provide an important food source for animals such as the endangered Baw Baw frog and the mountain pygmy possum. Without these moths, many animals in this ecosystem would starve.

Alpine Tundra

Higher than 9,843 feet (3,000 m) above sea level, temperatures drop to a point where the mountain environment becomes more like **Arctic tundra**. There, only the toughest plants and animals survive. Mosses and **lichens** cover the rocks. Flowers must bloom quickly to take advantage of the short summer. These plants tend to be small, and grow in rocky places that protect them from the wind. The flowers and mosses provide food for insects, which are food for spiders and birds.

Alpine tundra can look bare compared to the ecosystems at lower elevations, but flowers, mosses, and lichens provide food to animals even here.

A Source of Cold Water

Mountain tundra can be important to the ecosystems lower down the mountain. Animals such as the woodland caribou, the chinchilla of the Andes, and the kea parrot from New Zealand visit from lower elevations. There are fewer predators on the mountain tundra, so it is easier for animals to survive there.

On mountain tundra, most of the moisture falls as snow. Temperatures are so cold that the snow can last year-round. In some areas, snow freezes into large sheets of ice called **glaciers**. In these glaciers, mountains can store water for centuries. As the glaciers slowly melt, they release water into mountain streams that feed rivers farther downstream. Some of the biggest rivers in the world, including the Saskatchewan River in Canada, are fed by **meltwater** from mountain glaciers.

Eco Up Close

The sky pilot is a flower that blooms between 9,843 and 14,108 feet (3,000 and 4,300 m) above sea level in the Sierra Nevada Mountains. This plant has adapted to survive intense sunlight, drying winds, and freezing nights by insulating itself, or keeping warm, in a thick cover of leaves. It is a perennial, meaning it blooms each year. However, it blooms for just one day in summer. High on the mountain tundra, there are only a few insects that can **pollinate** the plant, so the sky pilot's bright flowers and strong scent make it easier for insects to find.

sky pilot

Plateaus and Montane Steppes

Some mountain ecosystems can be larger than just one single mountain. There are parts of Earth where the crust has pushed up so much that large areas are at a high elevation. Examples include the Ethiopian Highlands in East Africa and the Tibetan Plateau within the Himalayas.

As with normal grasslands, plateaus offer a lot of space for herbivores to roam and find food, but the animals must be adapted to the cold conditions.

The Roof of the World

The Tibetan Plateau is called "the Roof of the World." It stretches nearly 621 miles (1,000 km) north and south, and 1,553 miles (2,500 km) east to west. It has an average elevation of nearly 14,731 feet (4,490 m) above sea level, higher than 10 Empire State Buildings stacked on top of each other. Due to its size, the Tibetan Plateau has large areas that are quite flat.

The elevation makes the Tibetan Plateau too cold for trees to grow. The surrounding mountains block most clouds and keep the area dry. Less than 12 inches (300 mm) of moisture falls on this plateau, and it mostly comes in the form of hailstorms. The local habitat is mainly grassland or steppe. Plants and animals have to adapt to the thinner air (the air has a lower percentage of oxygen) on the Tibetan Plateau, but there is plenty of room for large groups of animals. This allows some herbivores, such as yaks and tahrs, to travel in herds, looking for food. Predators such as wolves and snow leopards hunt them. This leopard has developed the thickest coat of any big cat to keep warm in the cold Tibetan Plateau conditions.

Eco Up Close

Just as in the African savanna, the grasslands of the Tibetan Plateau have vultures. These birds are scavengers that help break down dead animals. This process helps decomposers return to the soil nutrients from the remains. The Himalayan vulture perches on the tall cliffs overlooking the plateau. It has a wingspan of up to nearly 10 feet (3 m), allowing it to soar above the landscape. A group of these vultures can strip all the meat off a dead yak in just two hours! The vultures have adapted to take advantage of a food source in an energy-poor environment.

Himalayan vulture

The Death Zone

The higher the elevation of a mountain, the thinner the air, or the **atmosphere**, becomes. At 26,247 feet (8,000 m) above sea level, the air pressure is almost one third of what it is at sea level. It is difficult to breathe, and people's lungs do not take in enough oxygen to survive. People climbing above this level must carry an oxygen tank. Without it, they will get **hypoxia**, or altitude sickness. When that happens, they feel tired and light-headed. They can become confused, have **hallucinations**, and pass out. In extreme cases, people can die within minutes.

Extreme Living

A lack of oxygen is not the only problem the higher a person travels. The thin atmosphere also lets through more of the sun's harmful ultraviolet rays. Winds can blow at more than 186 miles per hour (300 kph), and the temperatures can drop below −40 degrees Fahrenheit (−40 °C).

Very high up on a mountain, the only organisms that can live are called **extremophiles**. These are tiny plants, animals, or bacteria adapted to survive in extreme conditions. An example is tardigrades, also known as waterbears. These are **microscopic** animals that eat plant or bacteria cells, and sometimes other tardigrades. They can survive some of the hottest and coldest conditions on the planet, and have even survived in space.

Eco Focus

Permafrost is loose rock or soil that is held together by water that stays frozen all year round. It exists in tundra ecosystems and in the death zone at the top of mountains. Climate change is already threatening to melt the permafrost of the Arctic. What could happen to a mountain ecosystem if its permafrost melts?

More than 3,100 people have tried to climb Mount Everest. Of those people, more than 220 have died attempting to reach the top.

Eco Up Close

Living at elevations as high as 21,982 feet (6,700 m) above sea level, the Himalayan jumping spider may be one of the highest-living animals on the planet. While very little else lives around it, the spider still manages to find food. It eats insects such as springtails and flies, that are blown up the mountain on the wind. It is the **apex predator** of its small ecosystem.

Himalayan jumping spider

Mountains of the Sea

Some of the tallest mountains on Earth cannot be seen. Seamounts are mountains that rise at least 984 feet (300 m) above the sea floor. These are usually volcanoes, most of them extinct. An example includes the Bowie Seamount, found 112 miles (180 km) west of the coast of northern British Columbia. There may be as many as 100,000 seamounts in the oceans of the world.

Mixing Things Up

Just as mountains change wind **currents**, seamounts change water currents. Water moving along the bottom of the sea is pushed up the side of the seamounts, mixing with other currents and stirring up **sediments**. This provides food for plankton, which are microscopic algae that grow in the sunlit zone of oceans. The plankton are eaten by small fish and crabs, which in turn are eaten by larger animals, such as sharks, whales, and sea turtles that visit from the open ocean.

Seamounts can be important feeding and **breeding grounds** for many of the ocean's plants and animals. They can also help coral reefs grow. The food found around seamounts can also feed seabirds that fly above the ocean surface.

Coral reefs are among the most diverse ecosystems on the planet. This means that they contain many different **species**.

Eco Focus

It is easy to drag a fishing net across an ocean floor, but it is hard to visit the ocean floor to explore it. Only 350 of the world's 100,000 seamounts have been studied. What makes studying the world's seamounts more difficult than fishing on them? How might this affect our efforts to protect their ecosystems?

Eco Up Close

The Australian orange roughy is a fish that is found in the deep waters off Australia and New Zealand. It lives in **ocean canyons** and around seamounts, where it finds food in the mix of water and sediments there. In turn, the fish is food for sharks, eels, and mackerels. The fish lives for up to 150 years and is slow to grow and breed, which makes it difficult for the species to recover after **overfishing**. Since the fish was discovered in the 1970s, 90 percent of its population has vanished as a result of overfishing.

Australian orange roughy

Mountains and Other Ecosystems

As well as affecting the ecosystems around them, mountains also affect our planet's climate. Mountains are the source of rivers that carry water to ecosystems thousands of miles away. They are also barriers that block winds and change their direction. By doing so, they change Earth's climate.

Wet and Dry

Warm, moist air that blows in from the Pacific Ocean is forced to climb the mountains along the west coast of North America. The air cools as it rises, until it can no longer hold onto its moisture, which then falls as rain or snow. This feeds the cloud forests and coastal forests on the sides of the mountain near the ocean.

Once over the other side of the mountain, called the leeward side, the air falls. As it falls, it becomes warmer and creates hot, dry winds. In Alberta, these are called Chinook winds, or "snow eaters." In Argentina, they are called Zonda winds. On the leeward side of the mountain, less rain falls. This is why the wide grasslands of the Canadian and American prairies are found east of the Rocky Mountains, where it is dry. They are in the mountains' **rain shadow**.

Bringing the Monsoons

The Himalaya Mountains keep cold Arctic air from reaching India. This makes the country's northern regions warmer than other places at the same latitude. The mountains also block warm, wet air from the south. This forces the air to rise so moisture in clouds turns to raindrops, producing enormous rainstorms called monsoons. India depends on the monsoons to water its crops, but the monsoons also cause floods that damage crops and disrupt people's lives.

Mountain glaciers around the world hold nearly 40,785 cubic miles (170,000 cubic km) of ice. Meltwater from these glaciers feeds many of our largest rivers.

Eco Up Close

The porcupine is a common herbivore found across North America from Alaska to Mexico. The animals are excellent tree climbers, and are often found in forests. They have also adapted to live in tundras, deserts, and on mountains up to 12,139 feet (3,700 m) above sea level. Porcupines are well known for their quills, which are hardened, spiky hairs that can hurt predators that try to eat the animal. Along with being well protected, the porcupine can eat almost any plant. Both these features help it live in many different ecosystems.

porcupine

People and Mountains

George Mallory, one of the first British citizens to try to climb Mount Everest, was asked why he wanted to climb the mountain. He famously replied, "Because it's there." Throughout history, mountains have had a great impact on human lives.

Barriers to Conquer

Mountains often get in people's way. Before tunnels were built through mountains, mountain passes were the only way for people to travel across mountain ranges. The passes ensured people on either side of mountains could trade with each other. Many people also enjoy climbing mountains, pushing their bodies to the limit, and going where few other people can.

Tourism and Damage

Mountains are tourist attractions and many people visit to take part in snow sports. Resort towns such as Vail in Colorado and Banff in Alberta attract thousands of people each year. The stores, hotels, and houses built to serve these tourists can harm the very ecosystem these tourists want to see.

Protecting Mountains

Today, national parks have been set up to protect mountain ecosystems. Yellowstone National Park in the United States, Banff National Park in Canada, and the Great Himalayan National Park in India are examples of mountain national parks. These parks protect natural areas and limit hunting. They encourage visitors to clean up after themselves, and give the local plants and animals their space.

Everest base camp

Towns and cities built up around mountain resorts have reduced the habitat of local plants and animals.

Eco Up Close

Climbers have damaged Mount Everest. As many as 56 tons (50 MT) of garbage have been dumped on Mount Everest during the last 100 years. The cold and the lack of oxygen means this trash does not decompose. The government of Nepal has told people climbing Everest to bring all their garbage back with them, as well as at least an additional 17.6 pounds (8 kg) of previously left garbage.

Saving Mountains

Mountain ecosystems may be small, but they have a big impact on the environment around them. Mountain glaciers bring water to lands thousands of miles away. Mountains are home to plants and animals, such as the mountain lion shown below, that are found nowhere else on the planet. They also provide breeding grounds for many other organisms from other ecosystems.

However, climate change and pollution are threatening mountain ecosystems across the world. It is up to us to save the mountains of the world.

What Can You Do?

Write to your politicians and tell them to protect mountain ecosystems from **development**.

Do not leave taps running when you are not using the water, and buy **low-flow** toilets and showerheads. If we have more water to go around, we are less likely to take it from the mountains.

Turn off lights when you do not need them, use cars less, and walk more to reduce the need for fossil fuels and electricity. This helps limit climate change.

Activity:
Wind and Water Currents

Build your own wind tunnel to find out for yourself how mountains affect air and water currents.

Instructions

1. Take a large cardboard box that is open at the top. Have an adult use the box cutters to cut a large viewing window at one end of the box.
2. Cover the viewing window with the plastic sheet, fixing it in place with tape.
3. Place a fan at the end of the box opposite the viewing window. Make sure the air blows into the box.
4. Tape the air filter in the middle of the box, in front of the fan.
5. Build your mountain using construction paper. Place it at the back of the box, opposite the fan.
6. Turn on the fan and let it run for a few minutes.
7. Have an adult light the candle, let it burn for a few minutes, then blow it out. While the candle is still smoking, hold it inside the box between the air filter and the mountain.
8. Observe how the smoke moves over the mountain.
9. Repeat while holding the smoking candle at different positions, lower on the mountain, or higher. How do the air currents behave? Record your observations.

smoke

viewing window

The Challenge

Once your experiment is complete, present it to others and discuss the following questions:

- What happens if you change the shape of the mountain?
- What happens if you add more mountains?

Glossary

Please note: Some bold-faced words are defined in the text

abiotic factors Nonliving parts of an ecosystem, such as water and soil

adapt Change over long periods of time or many generations to better survive an environment

algae A group of organisms that have chlorophyll and can make their own food, but are not plants

apex predator A carnivore at the top of the food chain, which has few, if any, predators of its own

Arctic tundra An ecosystem found close to the north or south pole with short, cool summers and long, very cold winters

atmosphere The layer of gases that surrounds the surface of Earth

bacteria Living organisms made up of only one cell

biodiversity The variety of plant and animal life in an ecosystem or other area on Earth

biotic factors Living parts of an ecosystem, such as plants and animals

breed To produce offspring

breeding grounds Special places where animals produce offspring

carbon dioxide The gas that living things breathe out

chlorophyll A green substance in plants that changes sunlight and carbon dioxide into energy, which is stored as sugar and used by the plant for food

climate change A process in which the environment changes to become warmer, colder, drier, or wetter than normal. This can be caused by human activity

condense When a vapor cools and comes together into a liquid

coniferous A group of evergreen trees with needle-shaped leaves that develop cones for seed production

currents Movements of water or air in the same direction

dams Structures that block the flow of water in a river or stream

deciduous Describing a type of tree with leaves that grow in the spring and the summer and are dropped in the fall

development Changing natural lands to fit the needs of people by building structures and making areas for them to use

fertile Having or capable of producing a lot of vegetation

food chain A chain of organisms in which each member uses the member below as food

food web The interlinked food chains in an ecosystem

fungi Organisms, such as mold, that absorb food from their environment

glaciers Slow-moving masses of ice

greenhouse gases Additional gases in the air, such as carbon dioxide or methane, which trap the sun's heat in the atmosphere and keep it from being reflected out into space

habitat The natural environment of an animal or plant

hallucinations Visions that are not real

hypoxia When a person does not have enough oxygen in his or her body to survive

interrelationships The relationships between many different organisms and their environment

keystone species A species that plays such an important role in its environment that it affects many other organisms

lichens Types of organisms made up of fungi and algae, living together in a mutualistic relationship

low-flow Not using as much water as normal

meltwater Water from melted snow or ice, such as glaciers

microscopic So small that it can be seen only through a microscope

migrate To travel in regular patterns for food or to reproduce

mosses Small plants that grow on damp ground and do not have flowers or roots

mutualistic relationship A close relationship between two or more species that benefits or helps both species

nutrients Substances that allow organisms to thrive and grow

ocean canyons Places in the ocean where the floor drops considerably below the surrounding area

organisms Living things

overfishing Taking too many fish for food

overgrazing When animals eat more grasses than the ecosystem can replace

plates Portions of Earth's crust that float on top of its mantle

pollinate To transfer pollen grains to the part of a plant that can reproduce

predators Animals that hunt other animals for food

rain shadow An area that is downwind from the mountain and gets very little rain

sediments Dirt, sand, or soil that is carried away by fast-moving water, and falls to the bottom of a body of water when the flow slows down

shrubs Shorter plants such as bushed with many woody stems or trunks

silt Fine sand or clay that is easily carried along by running water

species A group of animals or plants that are similar and can produce young

subspecies A group of animals that shares the same characteristics and can breed with other animals of the same species, but are different from the main species

temperate A temperature that is not too hot, and not too cold

Learning More

Find out more about Earth's precious mountain ecosystems.

Books

Fabiny, Sarah. *Who Was Rachel Carson?* New York, NY: Grosset & Dunlap, 2014.

Harris, Tim. *Mountains and Highlands* (Biomes Atlases). Chicago, IL: Raintree, 2010.

Hurley, Michael. *The World's Most Amazing Mountains* (Landform Top Tens). Chicago, IL: Raintree, 2010.

Hyde, Natalie. *Conquering Everest* (Crabtree Chrome). Toronto, Canada: Crabtree Publishing Company, 2013.

Websites

Find out more about foothills at this website:
www.foothillsrestorationforum.ca

This U.S. National Park Service's website gives an introduction to mountain ecosystems:
www.nps.gov/noca/naturescience/bio-diversity1.htm

The Kids Do Ecology website has several pages about Alpine biomes at:
http://kids.nceas.ucsb.edu/biomes/alpine.html

Visit the WWF–Mountain Habitats pages to learn how mountains are created, what plants and animals live there, and what the WWF is doing to protect these ecosystems:
www.worldwildlife.org/habitats/mountains

Index